NLP for Teens

Judy Bartkowiak

2

<u>ABOUT THE AUTHOR</u>

As you can see from the photo, Judy is not a teenager. But then J.K. Rowling isn't a wizard!

Judy Bartkowiak is an NLP (Neuro Linguistic Programming) Master Practitioner with specialised training in working with teens. She is passionate about introducing NLP to a younger generation both directly or by teaching it to parents and teachers. She runs a therapy practice in the UK and offers consultation across the world via Skype and telephone.

Judy says, "My oldest children were in their early teens when I was first introduced to NLP by Sue Knight. I started implementing the principles immediately and was amazed that even as an NLP novice, which I then was, it could make huge differences both to the outcomes and more importantly at the time, to my state of mind. My kids started picking up the NLP as I modelled it for them and even used it themselves on their friends.

The teen years are, I feel, the most challenging for parents, teens and teachers yet potentially the most exciting and rewarding as our children develop from caterpillar to butterfly; from awkward adolescent to elegant adult.

Ever since I was first introduced to NLP by Sue Knight, (author of NLP at Work and an NLP Trainer), I have been guided by NLP principles as a parent and found them to bring about truly remarkable results."

Judy qualified in Neuro Linguistic Programming in 2001 and then took Open University qualifications in Creative Writing. She has written children's books as well as her Engaging NLP series and a Teach Yourself book 'Be a happier parent with NLP'.

If you'd like to ask Judy about your teens issue, be trained in NLP or arrange a coaching session for your child or teenager, email her at judy@nlpkids.com.

ENGAGING NLP

Neuro Linguistic Programming is a way of life, a new and different, positive approach to the way we communicate and how we interpret the way others communicate with us both verbally and non-verbally.

The only way to make effective changes in our life is to engage with this new NLP way and incorporate it daily into everything we do.

At home, at work or at play, whether we are a child, a teenager or an adult, we can make new choices about how we live our life so that we achieve all we wish for in our friendships, relationships and our own state of well-being and happiness.

Engage with NLP and you will see, hear and feel the difference immediately.

CONTENTS

INTRODUCTION

NLP is a completely different approach to life. Once you start reading the first chapter which contains the key principles, it will all make sense to you. This is because it is so logical and positive.

John Grinder and Richard Bandler developed what they came to call NLP from a combination of Virginia Satir's Family Therapy, Fritz Perls' Gestalt Therapy and the work of Milton Erickson in the area of language patterns.

What Grinder and Bandler developed from these was the idea of coding excellence. They studied how successful and effective people communicated. Then they came up with some ground rules that would bring these results to anyone who applied them. These ground rules are what we call NLP or Neuro Linguistic Programming 'presuppositions'.

This book is designed first and foremost to be a practical workbook for you to use, write in and apply on a day to day basis.

NLP BASICS

NLP has a number of principles that form the basis for all the practical techniques that you will learn in this book.

I find that if I get stuck, just by applying one of these rules I can find a solution. Each rule makes you stop and think differently about what isn't working for you so you can change it.

NLP is about setting positive outcomes or goals, working out the positive intention from every behaviour and learning from the feedback. The focus is on what you <u>do</u> want, rather than what you don't want.

1) If you always do what you've always done

then you will always get what you've always got

This is a great one to start with because it really challenges us to initiate change.

What it means is that if the result you are getting, whether that be in your personal life, at home or at school is not what you want then you must change your <u>own</u> behaviour in order to get a different result.

How often do we just keep on doing what we've always done and hope that eventually the result will be different. We blame other people; the teacher, our parents, lack of money, our boyfriend/girlfriend but ultimately it's up to us to do something different to get the result we want.

It's important to have a desirable outcome in mind for every situation. For example, I had a consultation the other day with a girl who is taking her GCSEs this year. "I hope I do well", she said. We worked together on a Time Line (this is covered later in the book) and once she recognised how much she wanted to be a PE teacher she realised she had a specific desirable outcome of getting a B in Maths that she would need to pursue her career. What she was doing at the moment would only get her a 'C', so we discussed what she could do differently in order to achieve the 'B' she wanted.

Passing an exam or getting a specific grade is quite a big desirable outcome but even in everyday situations such as a discussion with your teacher or doing your homework, negotiating a later bed time or permission to go to a party or club; these are all opportunities to establish before you start the conversation, what your desirable outcome is and how to communicate differently to get a more positive outcome.

So here is a new way of thinking.

Do something different.

If you do something different you will get a different result.

Think of a situation that occurs frequently that you'd like to change. Write it down here.

I want to change………..

Now think about what you would like to happen instead. What is your desirable outcome? Write that down now.

What I want to happen is………

Be specific and get to the detail. What <u>exactly</u> do you want, from whom, when and in what way? Write this down here.

I want ....

The more specific you can be about what you want to happen, the easier it will be to decide how to change what you are currently doing in order to achieve it.

What you do now to achieve your goals is dictated by your beliefs. The reason you do it is because you have a belief that this will work.

Our beliefs stems from our own early childhood and how we were brought up, what you consider to be of value and important to you. This may also have come from the culture you are from, the area or region and who you have grown up with.

If what you are doing is not working then look at the underlying belief behind this behaviour.

Are you sure your underlying belief is sound? Could you be carrying forward into the present a belief that belongs in the past?

Look back at the situation you have written about and list all the beliefs that affect your thinking. What beliefs do you have about what should happen in that situation?

I believe that...........

I believe that.............

I believe that..............

Where have your beliefs come from?

Are they valid for you today? Are they serving you well or making life more difficult?

Could you re-think a belief so that you could make other choices of behaviour?

Whenever you find yourself thinking 'I should do....' - change it to, 'I could do...' so that you give yourself permission to do something different.

Do your beliefs limit your choices of behaviour? Increase your options and change your behaviour to get the result you want.

Consider each option and how likely each one is to bring about the outcome you want.

This process requires that you step into the shoes of the other people involved in your situation rather than just look at it from your own perspective. This is an enormously powerful tool that you can learn now and apply throughout your life.

When you find yourself saying 'I can't do.....' ask yourself instead, 'and what if I could?' What difference would it make in your life if you could do the thing you believe you can't do? How about believing that you can do it, right now! Act as if you can, visualise that you can and you're already there.

2) *You have the resources to do whatever you want to do*

You have a huge resource of skills that you have been building since you were small. Each one, when applied in different contexts gives you yet more skills and options.

Lots of teenagers think that they have no skills but that is not so. In the hurly burly of teenage years it's easy to feel overwhelmed and feel we can't cope.

So if you are feeling a low sense of self belief, imagine that someone else is watching you over the course of the day. What would they observe? What would they see you do?

What you do automatically or unconsciously is a skill that someone else observing would admire. Pretend you are someone who doesn't know you, observing all you do.

- Look at each thing you do over the course of the day and write down the skill you use to do that thing. Make a list here.

- What do you believe about doing this thing? How important is the way you do it? How well do you feel you do this thing?

The reason I do………………………………

well is because I believe…….

The reason I do………………………………

well is because I believe…….

The reason I do………………………………

well is because I believe…….

15

The reason I do................................

well is because I believe........

Now list each thing you do well and give each
one a score out of 10 for how important it is to
you to do this thing well.

1.

2.

3.

4.

5.

- Now look at each thing you do and ask yourself, 'What does that <u>also</u> mean I can do?'

  Write that down in a list here. You may be surprised at how you can use a skill in many different parts of your life.

- When you are struggling

  - identify the skill you need

  - think about when and where you had that skill

  - ask yourself, what was the belief you had that enabled you to use that skill

  - accept that belief now in order to access the skill.

When we talk about accepting or taking on a belief in NLP we mean that we change our belief. A belief is not a value. A value is a moral code you live by and that is not likely to change as it was instilled in you as a child and is governed by both your upbringing and your environment.

A belief is something you hold to be true about the things you do and they change as you experience new situations and people. For example, you certainly hold different beliefs now from those you held as a child such as believing in Father Christmas or the Tooth Fairy!

In my work with teenagers I've heard lots of beliefs that are very limiting

What are your limiting beliefs? What are the things you think you 'can't' do? Write them here.

Think of a time when you didn't have that belief. What was different then?

What could you do then, what skills did you have then or in that situation that you need to have now?

Write them down here:

You still have that skill so use it to change those limiting beliefs of yours and get a different result.

3) If someone else can do it you can too

This is a very empowering belief to take on board as a teenager, isn't it? How often do we see other people do things that we admire and would like to do ourselves?

If you have noticed a skill in someone else, the chances are that in some way you too have this skill because that is how you come to have noticed it in the first place. We say 'if you spot it, you've got it!'

You can acquire these new skills and hone existing ones by modelling (or copying) it in someone who demonstrates that skill with excellence.

How do we do it?

  a) First we need to identify the skill we want.

We do this by observation. Observe and be intently curious about what you see and how your model (the person you want the skill from) behaves.

Watch every part of the skill, the non-verbal cues such as body language and the verbal ones, the tone of voice, language patterns, volume and pace.

Identify which part of the skill you need because it is unlikely you need all of it.

Decide which bit you need and break it into small parts that you can practice.

b) Think about the belief your model would have in order to use that skill.

Do this by reflecting 'If I did that, I would be thinking I was ….'.

Perhaps your model sounds confident or calm, maybe looks fantastic or is getting good marks, has a fit boyfriend / girlfriend, is playing great sport?

Where in your life do you have that belief? Maybe you have that belief when you are doing something you love, playing a sport or with your friends?

Think hard about where you have the belief and visualise yourself in that situation where the belief is strong.

It's not unusual even in co-ed schools to find teens feel awkward around other teens of the opposite sex who they meet out of school. Use modelling to copy the way to mix more easily by noticing those who do it well. Be curious about their beliefs. Can you take on the belief that would enable you to feel more at ease?

c) Now practice the precise skill you have identified. You can do this on your own first and then practise on your friends.

Notice the results you get and keep practising until you get your desirable outcome.

It often takes a few different models of a skill to help you acquire it for yourself and use in a way that works for you.

Once you have mastered this modelling exercise you can use it to do other things you currently find hard.

Lots of teenagers want to get weekend and holiday jobs or you might have left school and are looking for your first job. Use modelling to get what you want. Find someone who has been successful and ask them what was in their mind when they applied and when they had their interview. Look at their CV, how could you use the same format or learn from what they wrote so you can improve on yours?

4) There is no failure only feedback

It's quite normal for teenagers to feel failures: actually it's not even an exclusive club! We all feel failures - sometimes even celebs.

Things don't always go as we'd like and when that happens we get upset and feel we've failed.

However, imagine you held a belief that there is no failure only feedback. How much more reassuring is that?

What can we learn from what went wrong so that there is a good positive outcome?

Scientists spend their life doing experiments, recording what they did and what happened. It can take many many attempts to get it right. They don't give up do they? They view each attempt as a step towards success, learning as they go.

When you were a baby you would have made many attempts before you were able to stand up holding onto something and then standing up alone and then walking, then running. You didn't give up or think you'd failed.

As you go through these teen years you will make loads of mistakes and this is how you learn what works and what doesn't. Don't beat yourself up each time you make a mistake but learn from it and do it differently next time.

You can't exist without communicating; whether that is verbal or non verbal communication, simply by 'being' you are communicating a message.

For example, when adults look across the road and see a teenager, they notice your clothes, hair, body language and maybe hear what you are saying.

They don't know you and they haven't had any interaction with you but already they have a response.

The response we feel and the response we get from others is a result of our communication in the same way. So we are communicating all the time and receiving communication back.

The communication we receive is feedback. The feedback can be verbal or non verbal and we can use it to learn more about what and how we are communicating.

How we choose to respond will be determined by our own beliefs and values.

There is no <u>one</u> correct or definitive response.

When someone responds negatively to you, including your teachers, parents and friends, remember that they are giving you feedback and you can choose to accept it or not, depending on whether it seems reasonable when set against your own beliefs and values.

Their feedback is not a fact of life but simply their opinion at that moment and this will be influenced by their beliefs and values, internal state or mood as well as yours, of course.

You may be getting negative feedback because someone is just in a bad mood, feeling rough, depressed, or cross about something unrelated that has happened to them.

You have two choices when you get negative feedback. You can choose to accept it or reject it.

Accept it if you think they may have a fair point and take the opportunity to reword what you said or do something differently. By doing this you are using the feedback as an adult learning experience that will enable you to communicate in rapport next time.

However difficult it might be at the time, if you believe they are being reasonable in their feedback, thank them for the feedback and do something different.

If however, when you reflect on what they said or their non verbal feedback, you decide that it is unreasonable then you can choose to ignore it or say that you don't agree with the negative feedback.

Instead of feeling you have failed when you get negative feedback, reframe this with its positive intention, which is for you to learn from it. Lots of teenagers suffer from depression. If you sometimes do too then give yourself a feedback sandwich.

1. *What did I do well?*

2. *What would make it <u>even</u> better next time?*

3. *What was good overall?*

We need to avoid:

a) Generalisations

These are when we complain that the teacher 'always' gives us a low mark or 'never' explains the homework clearly.

Perhaps we tell mum that 'everyone' goes out clubbing during the week or that 'no-one' is revising yet?

Generalisations are rarely true so they don't have much impact. In fact it's when you think of the exceptions that you learn something revealing. When was it not true? When did you get a good mark, what was different about what you did? When did you understand the homework, how was it different then?

b) Deletions

When we delete the context of feedback by being vague, it isn't very helpful. Saying 'that's better' or 'work harder' isn't specific and needs some detail. So ask for the detail from whoever is giving you feedback. If you are the one giving feedback, be specific.

c) Distortions

Sometimes we make assumptions about what our friends, parents or teachers are doing and why they are doing it. We might say, 'you're deliberately annoying me' or 'you're making me cross'. They aren't. This is not helpful as we are not mind readers so we are in effect distorting the facts.

What is really happening is that we are choosing to be cross or annoyed so we should tell them this instead and focus on the behaviour.

Be aware that drink and drugs create distortions and mess with your head. At the time, we think they make us happy and fun to be with and <u>this</u> is the distortion. Being happy is your choice – nothing <u>makes</u> you happy. Anything that affects your brain, limits your choices by distorting your judgement.

Challenge the beliefs you hear from your peers and check in with your own values. Trust your gut instincts and use internal representation to make your own judgements. Ask yourself 'And what do <u>I</u> think?' which is getting into 'adult mode'.

5) If you try, you won't succeed

How many times a day do we assure people that we will 'try' and do something? Why do we use that word 'try'?

I've heard this from teenagers I see at the clinic. They say they are 'trying' hard at school or 'trying' to behave better. It's because we know deep down that we may not actually have the time or inclination to do it.

Perhaps we think we don't have the skill? We want to keep our options open really, don't we? We don't want to give a promise that we may not be able to keep and we don't want to let people down.

We also don't want to say 'no' because that would appear confrontational or provoke further discussion which we don't have the time or desire to pursue. So off we go to 'try' and do that thing, knowing that we don't have to do it, we just have to 'try' to do it.

What does 'trying to do it' look like? Well it looks like someone accepting that they can't and won't do it fairly shortly after they've said they'll 'try'.

Perhaps our teachers urge us to 'just try your best'. Yet there is built-in failure in the word 'try'. Notice when you use this word and reword your sentence without the word 'try' so you will be more motivated. 'Try' presupposes you will find it difficult so you will give up on the exercise more quickly than if your expectation is that you could do it.

Imagine there are two boxes in front of you and I ask you to pick up the first one. You will pick it up quite easily because you assume it must be light.

Now I ask you to 'try' and pick up the other. Immediately you expect the other box to be heavier and you may have difficulty picking it up. If I then said, 'try hard' or 'just try it', I am emphasising the difficulty and you may look at it wondering how heavy it is and even consider asking for help. In fact the boxes are the same weight. The only difference is our expectations of how heavy the second box is.

There is built-in failure in the word 'try'. So if you are 'trying' to work hard, lose weight, give up smoking, get a job...............

Just 'do it'.

6) The map is not the territory

What this means is that how you see the world is different from how others see it. We all have different perceptions of our environment depending on our age, life stage, culture and experiences.

To assume our own perceptions are the only correct ones would in NLP terms be 'unecological'.

This is ever obvious when you consider how your parents see their world. Their map is very different from yours.

Their priorities are different and based on a much bigger map than yours because they have more responsibilities and may not remember how difficult it is to be studying or looking for a job.

Your map is smaller and more intense. This means that changes have more impact, whether that is a change of teacher, moving schools, or your parents splitting up

You fear change because so much is still unknown to you and you have limited experience to reassure you that it will be OK.

Whereas when adults encounter change they usually have something similar that they can draw on for reassurance and confidence.

If you have to make a significant change in your life either because you have made that choice or because it has been decided for you then remind yourself of other changes you have coped well with and take on the belief that you will be fine, just as you were last time.

7) The positive reframe

Often as teenagers we find ourselves doing things we don't want to do and may even feel resentful about.

Whatever we do though, we can look for the positive intention by reframing it or looking at it from another angle. Be creative and find some good things about what you don't like doing.

This is a great skill because it gives us control over our emotions and environment. Being able to put a positive gloss on unpleasant things will really help you through life.

The other way to use this skill is to reframe and look for the positive intention in your teacher or parent's behaviour. When they are doing or saying something you don't like, consider what positive intention they have for you.

Imagine yourself in their shoes. If you were doing or saying this, what might be the positive reason? Perhaps this is their reason too?

Once you understand their positive intention you can negotiate for what you want by offering them another way for them to get this. This way you have a 'win win'.

For example, if your parents want you to study for your exams rather than go out, the positive intention is for you to do well. Perhaps you could agree to do a few hours work before you go out?

Here's a really useful exercise for turning something that seems negative into a positive. It's called the SWISH pattern

1) What happens just <u>before</u> you get cross? This is called 'the trigger'. It's like a switch that we turn on in our head and 'bang' our mood changes. We need to change our reaction to the trigger.

   Is your trigger something you see (if you are visual) something someone says (if you are auditory) or something you feel (if you are kinaesthetic)?

   Write down what happens just <u>before</u> you feel bad or angry or sad.

The trigger for me is…………………….…..

Then what happens? Write it down here.

2) Make a picture in your head of what happens when you react really badly and imagine it like a picture on the screen as if it's a movie at the cinema.

3) Now think of what you would <u>like</u> to happen instead next time that trigger goes off in your head. Write it down in the box below.

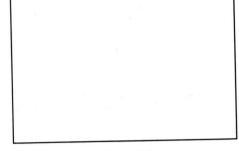

4) Make a picture in your head of this now. Then place that picture in the bottom left hand corner of the screen with your bad image in it. Like this.

5) Now say out loud 'SWISH' and make the good image in the corner switch with the bad image in the middle like this.

You will need to practice it a few times and when you have it perfect you can use it every time you see, hear or feel that trigger in your head.

This next section covers:

1. Identity - who are you?

2. Stress

3. Confidence

4. Relationships

5. Work

CHAPTER 2. IDENTITY

Who am I? This is a big question and one you need to know. You are making important decisions about your future as you choose GCSE options, A level subjects and University courses. How can you make these decisions if you don't know who you are?

Let's start with what is called in NLP your 'internal representation'. This is about how you see your world. There are 3; visual, auditory and kinaesthetic. Although you will use all three at different times, there will be one that tends to dominate and be your preferred system.

Read through them to decide which you are and then go back through to work out how those close to you process their world as it will help you to understand them better.

Here is a little quiz to help you.

Q1. You're watching a movie with some friends, what do you notice most?

    a) What the characters look like and what they are wearing

    b) The music, sound track and the voices

    c) Your own feelings, the emotion and the atmosphere

Q2. When you think about what you'll be doing next weekend, you

    a) Can picture yourself doing it

    b) Want to chat about it with your friends

    c) You feel excited already

Q3. If you have an argument with your parents you

    a) Look angry and take an aggressive stance

    b) Shout a lot

    c) Can be quite physical

Q4. After a holiday with friends you enjoy most

    a) Looking at the photos on Facebook

    b) Chatting about it

    c) Remembering how much fun it was and how you felt

Q5. You're looking for a weekend job. What's most important to you is

    a) What you will wear

    b) Who you can talk to there

    c) What the place will feel like to work in

Q6. On your mobile phone you spend more time

    a) Texting and looking at your photos

    b) Calling your friends

    c) Playing with the apps

Q7. Your favourite subjects at school are

    a) Anything arty

    b) Anything where there are discussions in class or anything musical

    c) Anything physical like sport or dancing

Q8. When you're feeling ill what concerns you most is

    a) What you look like

    b) What you sound like

    c) What you feel like

Q9. Thinking about your best mate…

    a) You look quite similar

    b) You talk about the same things

    c) You react the same way and do similar things

Q10. Your future job will be one which

    a) Is arty or creative in some way

    b) Is connected with music

    c) Is physical

A - Visual

If you answered mostly 'A's then you think in pictures and images, using expressions like 'do you see what I mean' or 'look at it from my point of view'.

You notice body language and facial impressions and may deduce a lot about a person before they've even spoken.

Visual people tend to speak quite quickly as they transpose the pictures in their head into words that almost tumble out in quick succession.

Your descriptions will have colour, brightness and texture and your surroundings will be important to you as will your appearance. You will (if you're allowed) have pictures and photos all over the wall of your room and you will have made choices about the colours in it.

Your clothes will be very important and you will always be on the look-out for new clothes that capture the look you're after. You'll enjoy flicking through magazines for ideas about fashion and notice what the celebs are wearing.

You'll probably enjoy programmes on TV about how people look and makeover programmes. You'll spend ages getting dressed and made up and would rather be late than go out without make up.

Boys, you too can be visual and you care how you look. Your emphasis may be on your body and muscles, building up that 6 pack and impressing the girls with your physique.

You can't wait to drive and what your first car looks like will be more important than what is under the bonnet. Colour, lines and style will be considered at length.

If you recognise yourself as visual then be aware that you will learn best from seeing rather than hearing so make notes in class because you'll remember what you see in your notes much better than what you remember being said.

You will find graphs and diagrams helpful so when you're revising, make mind maps, flash cards and represent visually whatever you can because it will stay in your head better like that. Tony Buzan is the name in mind mapping and as well as lots of excellent books he has software available that you can use to make your own mind maps. Flash cards are available on Amazon for almost every GCSE and A level subject and can be an excellent revision tool.

Use the Internet to aid your revision because you'll find the information presented visually and may even get to watch YouTube videos about your subject or videos. BBC Iplayer is another useful resource.

Use the local library for DVDs around your chosen subjects. They may not be on the shelf but librarians can get them ordered for you at a small cost.

Look for careers which focus on creative skills, appearance or style. It's hard to make a list but art and photography or jobs where it's important to see the bigger picture will feature on it.

Lots of visual people work for themselves as designers, architects, florists and so on.

B - Auditory

You are auditory if you enjoy music, notice the sounds around you and prefer your friends to call rather than text or email. You tend to remember what people say to you or what you've heard on the radio better than what you've read.

You might use expressions like 'did you hear what I said?' or 'shut up'.

An auditory teenager usually makes and enjoys a lot of noise and sounds are important to them. They will like singing, musical instruments and noisy video games.

You learn best by listening to the teacher rather than looking at what they've written on the board or asked you to read. You can assist your learning by saying over to yourself in your head what you are reading.

When you're revising, read out loud what you have in your notes and make use of any Internet sites that have sound.

Lots of auditory people like to work with someone else so they can discuss their work. Project work will suit you or ideally having a revision buddy who can ask you questions that you have to answer rather than write down.

You could read your notes into the voice memo on your phone or use programmes like audacity to record MP3 files. Then you can transfer them to your phone so you can listen to them rather than read them.

Check out podcasts and audiobooks to aid your learning as well as DVDs and Youtube videos.

For you, the sound of your ideal car will be what you notice and what people say about it. You probably want a car with a big noisy exhaust system and want a good sound system in the car.

Whilst good sounds attract you, discordant sounds will annoy, so other people's music that is not to your taste will be irritating as will noises of other people talking while you are trying to concentrate. You can manage that by using headphones with your own preferred music on while you are revising.

Good careers for auditory people would be anything involving music or jobs that require good listening and communicating skills.

C - Kinaesthetic

You are an active person and enjoy being on the go. Exercise and fitness is important to you and you like to have physical contact with your friends and your family.

You notice the temperature and feel uncomfortable if it's not right.

You may use expressions like 'let's get going' or 'that doesn't feel right' because you are very sensitive to atmosphere. You frequently talk in terms of 'I feel...' because for you this is your modus operandum.

A kinaesthetic teenager wants action. Sitting still isn't easy and they need to have things to do. Some kinaesthetic students walk around reciting their notes because this action enables them to focus. Studying is harder for you because it is too sedentary so break your study time up into small chunks and fit in your sport or go for short runs or cycles in between.

You prefer to be shown what to do rather than told and want to be actively participating in your learning. Project work will suit you as will interactive computer learning of which there are many on the Internet and on mobile phones.

Make notes when you are listening and use highlighters to emphasise words or phrases because for you, active listening works best.

You will be conscious of the atmosphere in the room and will find it hard to work if you aren't in the right frame of mind. Take time to organise yourself so you are comfortable and at the right temperature before you start work.

Careers that will suit you best are active jobs with plenty going on around you so anything connected with sport or physical jobs such as construction or a trade such as decorating or gardening will suit your preference.

In addition to the VAK (Visual, Auditory and Kinaesthetic) as we call the internal representational systems, there are also meta programs which filter what we see hear and feel.

There are a number of them but the most useful are:

<u>Small chunk/Big chunk</u>

Some of us like detail and for <u>all</u> the information to be made available to us. Whereas others prefer just the broad outline or the big picture. You can tell quickly which someone is by asking them a question such as 'what did you get up to last weekend?' The 'small chunker' will give you every last detail whereas the 'big chunker' will just tell you the basics 'great man really cool'.

If you are small chunk you'll find it easy to take on board maths and science subjects where accuracy and thoroughness are important. You will be good at remembering dates and facts in other subjects but subjects that are more analytical or broad brush such as philosophy or religious studies may prove more taxing.

The 'big chunker' is not fussed about accuracy so long as they understand the overall concept which may work in subjects that lend themselves to analytical thinking but won't work if there is a definite right or wrong answer.

If you are small chunk, select a topic area within a subject to revise and put everything else away out of sight. If you are big chunk you could tackle a subject and not feel overwhelmed.

When you need to chunk up to get the big picture ask yourself 'yes and what does that mean?' If you want to chunk down ask yourself 'how do I know this, what is the evidence, how did I get there?'

Choices/Process

Some people love choices and options. They take their time making decisions about everything and consider all available possibilities. This is fun for them.

Others just have a plan and want to get on with it, mentally ticking off the list what they need to do.

If you're revising or tackling homework, spending ages deciding which subject to work on first, whether to have a cup of tea or coffee, a sandwich or toast, isn't going to get anything done. If you are a choices person you may just have to limit your choices and start!

Internal/External referencing

You are externally referenced if you are easily influenced by what your friends say. For example, if they say they haven't started revision yet and you decide not to do any. An internally referenced person will decide for themselves when would be a good time to start and just get on with it.

It can be very useful as a teenager to be able to switch from external to internal referencing because this is a good way to protect yourself from bullying and peer group pressure.

Here's how to do it:

Imagine you can float out of your body and look at what is going on from the outside, like a webcam. What can that webcam see, hear and feel? Is what is being proposed reasonable?

Being totally internally referenced is of course untenable because someone who had no care at all about what other people thought would be very unpopular.

The ideal situation is for you to ask yourself 'what do I think about this?', ' how does it fit with what I value?' As you do that, you check in with your internal referencing system.

Towards/away from

Some people are focussed on what they want out of life, what we call our desirable outcome or goals. Others are more focussed on what they want to avoid. For example, weight loss is an 'away from' goal as it's couched in terms of what we don't want.

If you are revising because you want to pass your exam; then that's being 'towards'. Whereas if you're revising so you don't fail, then that's 'away from'.

If you think you are 'away from' then ask yourself 'what DO I want?'

SUMMARY

Knowing how you process information and how you learn best is a great way to improve your school and home life because it puts you in control. Knowledge is power!

You may need to revisit this chapter later when we look at relationships and work so make a note here about which you are.

VISUAL

AUDITORY

KINAESTHETIC

BIG CHUNK/SMALL CHUNK

CHOICES / PROCESS

INTERNAL/EXTERNAL REFERENCE

TOWARDS/ AWAY FROM

CHAPTER 3. STRESS

Let's face it; your parents have forgotten how stressful these teen years can be. Just at the very time they trust you out of their sight and you have some independence at last, school expects you to be working hard and worse still, taking exams.

One of the reasons that parents and teachers don't remember being 'stressed' is that it is a relatively new word, as is 'chilled'. The word your parents will have used is 'pressure' which has completely different overtones.

Pressure is a force acting either within us because we are putting the pressure on ourselves or it can be external where someone else, usually your teacher or parent, is putting the pressure on <u>you</u>.

Stress, on the other hand is more about how you respond to that pressure. We all experience stress because we all experience pressure but we react differently so our stress will not be the same as our friends. What is too much stress for you may be fine for your friend and you may be surprised at how he freaks out at something you take in your stride.

The problem at school is that stress is contagious. It is like a flu germ. A few people get it and pass it on to all their friends. It can be like that for you at home too. Mum keeps nagging you about the exams, reminds you how little time you've got and how much you have to do. She's stressed and she's passing it on to you. You don't need that. Pressure is fine but you don't want to take on other people's stress.

In fact, many people say that they work best under pressure. When time's short and deadlines loom, many people find they can be more charged up, more focussed and produce better work than when they sit at the computer distracted by Facebook and their phone.

First decide how you work best. Do you like to get work done in plenty of time so you can relax or are you best under pressure?

So the question for us is this….how can we manage the stress in such a way that we can take the positive aspects of pressure and minimise the negative consequences.

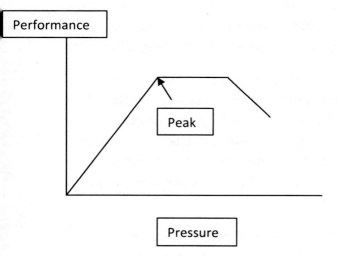

The simplified graph on the previous page shows that for most people, their performance improves as the pressure increases. This accounts for the symptoms of being scared and excited being very similar. When you are just about to go on an exciting scary ride at a theme park the feelings you experience are similar to the feeling you get just before you go into an important exam.

During that build up time you are maximising the positive force of the pressure and using it to produce results – performance. You are managing the stress and functioning effectively.

However, there comes a point when it all goes pear shaped and we can't take any more. We have perhaps not picked up on our body's signals to eat, rest, take a break or exercise and now productivity falls away after plateauing for a bit. There is a limit to how much pressure we can take.

The key to handling stress, is to be aware of when you are no longer managing the pressure effectively.

So what are the signs of stress?

1. If you can't sleep.

If you're having trouble sleeping at night that is a sure sign of stress.

You need your sleep so that your body can function properly and recover ready for the next day. We all need different amounts of sleep but we do all need to switch off completely and relax for at least 5 hours. There's plenty of evidence in fact that teenagers need 8 or 9 hours sleep, so make sure you get it . That doesn't mean texting your friends during the night!

2. If you're getting ill all the time.

If you're catching every bug going round, this is your immune system not being able to protect you because you're run down and stressed.

3. If you're getting irritable and snappy with your mates and your family.

4. If you can't concentrate.

5. If you just can't step back, prioritise and make good decisions.

This could include self-harming, drinking heavily, taking drugs or driving dangerously.

If you are experiencing any of these signs or several of them then you are not managing your stress and are already on the downward phase of the graph.

So how do we avoid this happening in the first place and what can you do about it right now.

1. The first thing to do is to recognise the signs. Accept the situation as it is. This is feedback. These negative behaviours have a positive learning for you and you need to take action.

2. You need to release the emotional aspect of the stress. You have perhaps suppressed these negative emotions; so express your frustration and your feelings of despair . A good way of doing this is to write down how you feel.

Talking about your feelings with others may help but you'll find they give you their feelings back and their solutions. The solutions are within you. You have all the resources you need and you have the answers so get rid of all those unhelpful negative thoughts on paper. This is called 'freefall writing' and comes from the subconscious mind. It can be a great stress reliever.

You might find it easier to express these feelings as a picture instead. Do what feels right for you.

3. Now release the physical stress. Exercise is great for this. If you play a sport or like to go running then fit in an exercise break into your day. It gets the blood flowing, oxygen to your brain and a break for your eyes.

4. The next stage is called 'grounding' and it means getting back in touch with yourself and what's important to you. Do you have a favourite place to go or friends you haven't seen for ages? Facebook and texting is all very well but it doesn't replace the physical connection you experience with friends as you meet and have a laugh together.

These first four stages are the winding down cycle. The next four are about winding up.

1. Have a sense of purpose. Remind yourself about what you're doing this exam for. What will passing this exam mean to you and what you want to do in your life? What is important to you?

Sometimes we get on a treadmill of exams and then more exams without really thinking about where we are going. Where are you going?

2. Set goals. Be clear about what you're buying into. The more you are in control of your goals the more likely you are to achieve them and the less stress you will have.

3. Make plans for how to achieve your goals and make priorities, make choices. Perhaps you need to revisit the identity chapter to understand how you learn best?

4. This last stage is the 'action' stage and is about achieving what you want in life.

Notice where you are in the process at the moment and get back in touch with your mind and body. They are 'one' and how you feel in your mind is reflected in your body and vice versa. This is called monitoring your state.

CHAPTER 4. CONFIDENCE

Firstly, let me assure you that you have all the resources you need already but you may need some help from NLP in finding them.

Let's start by making a list of all the things you can do well. Do this on the next page.

Write down first all the things you know you do well in any part of your life. We're not just focussing on school here.

Then write down all the things your friends would reckon you do well. Sometimes it helps to disassociate which means to imagine you are talking to your friends and they are telling you what they think you do well.

Include last what your family think you do well.

What I do well

Look at that list and tick the things that are important to you, things that you value. Then thinking about each of those ticked skills, think about what that also means you can do.

For example, I saw a young lad who reckoned he had no concentration and was easily distracted at school in lessons. While we were chatting it became clear that he had amazing concentration when it came to mastering a new PlayStation game and would sit for hours working his way up the levels until he'd completed them all - even if that took him all night!

We then used anchoring to access that concentration so he could apply it to his schoolwork.

Here's how we do anchoring.

Your anchor could be an image or a picture (if you are visual), a sound or piece of music (if you are auditory) or an action (if you are kinaesthetic).

Choose an anchor that you can easily access anywhere because you need it to be something that doesn't draw attention to yourself in a social situation.

Good anchors are natural actions such as picturing a scene or a painting if you are visual, quietly humming some bars of music if you are auditory or squeezing your ear lobe if you are kinaesthetic.

People in business and on the sport's field use anchors when they want to access a particular strength; confidence, calm, energy, focus. You can have different anchors for different strengths.

You may already have some unconscious anchors. Some may work well for you such as the sight of your girlfriend or boyfriend, the music of your favourite TV programme or the smell of supper.

Others may not work so well such as the sight of a particular teacher or the Head wanting to speak to you.

Use a conscious anchor to over-ride the unconscious one.

Step 1 – Establishing the anchor

Close your eyes and think about when and where you feel calm and relaxed, strong and in control. Picture yourself there in that situation.

What can you see? Give the scene colour and clarity. Turn up the brightness and focus on everything in your picture.

What can you hear? Is there music? What are people saying?'

What are you doing? What is happening? Is it hot or cold? How do you feel?

When you really feel associated into the situation and are as calm and confident as you could possibly be, fire the anchor. Do the thing you have decided to do as your anchor.

Step 2 – Break state

Think of something else for a moment just to relieve the tension. If you are visual, look at something else. If you are auditory hum a tune and if you are kinaesthetic, walk about for a minute.

Step 3 – Fire it again

Repeat step 1 and again make the images, sounds and feelings very strong before you fire the anchor.

Step 4 – Break state

Change your state for a minute – shake yourself or move about a bit.

Step 5 – Fire it again

Repeat the process. It will probably be quite quick by now.

Now you have your anchor, use it whenever you need that resource. You can establish different anchors for other resources.

When do we use it ?

The metaphor of an anchor is very appropriate because when we feel adrift, lost, confused and overwhelmed it is helpful to put down an anchor to stabilize ourselves and find a calm place in our mind and body. We can rely on the anchor because it is heavy and solid and it won't let us down.

From there we can access our resources to move forward in what we're doing. We use anchoring to achieve a sense of control and resourcefulness in any situation.

Another reason to anchor is that sometimes we need to remind ourselves of good times to help us through more challenging times.

The sense of calm you get from anchoring can help you find that inner strength when and where you need it. You can anchor anywhere at any time and it takes seconds.

Another good way to find the resource you need for a challenging situation is to use the Time Line.

This is an imaginary line along the floor that represents time from, at one end, the past through to the future at the other end.

After you've done it once you'll find all sorts of occasions to use a time line.

They're great for getting things into perspective when you feel a bit lost and lacking direction. If you've lost sight of your purpose you can walk back along the time line and find it to re-energise your goals.

If you find yourself saying 'I can't do…', use the Time Line to find out where that limiting belief came from. A limiting belief is something you think you can't do such as giving a talk to the whole school or going for a job interview, sitting a difficult exam.

When you experience grief or loss, whether that is for a person or a part of your life, you can travel back along the time line, find it and bring the parts you need now into the present.

Once you've done the Time Line a few times it will be in your head and you can conjure up the image and the steps without moving. This can be useful in situations when you can't actually move physically.

We can combine the Time Line with anchoring by firing our anchor at significant points along the line as triggers for change and to help us access a feeling of confidence in the future as we mentally time travel. This is particularly useful for grief.

Step 1- Associate into it

Imagine a line along the floor representing your life. Now stand at the point representing today, the present.

What do you see in your life? What images come to the fore? Who do you see? If you are visual, give this colour, tone and form like a painting or a photograph.

What do you hear? Who can you hear? Is there music? What sounds do you hear? If you are auditory make these into a full orchestra of sound.

What do you feel? Are you warm or cold? Who is touching you? What are you doing? If you are kinaesthetic really move with the feeling.

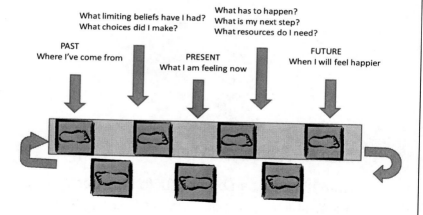

Step 2 – Move to where you will be happy

This move will take you to a point on the line when you will feel happier, have achieved what you desire or have reached some significant point on your life's journey.

Associate into this point as you did in Step 1

Step 3 – Move back to the present

In order to get to the desired point, things have to happen so what are the steps along the way to your goal? Walk through them one at a time, associating into each one.

Step 4 – Step back in time

Sometimes it can be helpful to step back along the time line if you find yourself saying 'I can't' or feel uncomfortable about something. By travelling back in time we can discover where these limiting beliefs came from and revisit them in terms of whether they serve us in our life now as a teenager.

By travelling back in time we can go to the point when we felt brave or had confidence, when we could negotiate or make friends easily.

Associate into those times in the past, anchor the skill and travel forward again back to the present and take them with you into your future.

I've taught lots of my teenage clients the Circle of Excellence which they use when they are tempted by friends to do things they'd rather not get into.

Imagine a circle on the ground in front of you. Think about how you want to feel – strong, calm, relaxed, confident, whatever.

Now think of a time when you were just like that and when the memory is really powerful, step into the circle. When it fades , step out again.

Think of another memory of that feeling you want to capture and again step into the circle when you've got it.

Do this a few times and then when you need that feeling step forward into your imaginary circle.

CHAPTER 5. RELATIONSHIPS

As you start having relationships with the opposite sex you will undoubtedly be discovering that they are not like us at all, are they?!

Girls can be evasive, unclear, not say what they mean so you have to play guessing games. You think everything is fine and then suddenly they dump you.

Boys don't talk or if they do it's about football and they don't tell you what they feel or what they want so you have to ask their mates which they really don't like.

Communication between boys and girls is tricky when you're in a relationship so apply the rules mentioned in the first chapter on identity.

1) Use their language pattern. Are they visual, auditory or kinaesthetic? For example;

"Shall we go to the cinema this weekend?' (kinaesthetic)

"Great, yes I'd like to go to the cinema I'll check what's on and text you back.' (kinaesthetic)

2) What's their meta-program – are they big chunk/small chunk, choices/process, towards/away from etc?

Match them. If they are process, don't give them loads of choices! If they are small chunk, break up your big idea into bite size chunks.

3) Virginia Satir explains that there are different behaviour types:

a) Blamer – aggressive, doesn't take responsibility for outcomes and typically says 'it's your fault'.

b) Placater – takes the blame for everything to keep the peace. Can't say 'no because you don't have any self esteem.

c) Leveller – bit of a computer, weighs everything up and takes a view but doesn't get emotionally involved.

d) Distracter – does anything for a laugh to avoid having to engage in the relationship.

Who are you in your relationship? It is not unusual for blamers and placaters to be drawn to each other and as you can imagine this would not be very healthy for either of them. If you are in this type of relationship, recognise it now. If you are the blamer, work on your rapport skills using the identity chapter and if you are the placate work on your confidence using that chapter.

Both leveller and distracters need to tune into their own feelings and start sentences with 'I feel...' and 'I want...' so that they connect with the people they are close to.

To aid rapport or 'getting along' with our friends we need to avoid the generalisations, distortions and deletions mentioned earlier in the book.

For example, comments like 'You always treat me badly' or 'You never text me' are unlikely to be true so notice when they do what you want and praise them for it so they get the message.

Mind reading by assuming their thoughts based on their behaviour is risky because we can't possibly know them that well so it's best to check it out; 'did you mean to ignore me in the bar/party/playground just then?'

Giving limited information is also quite complicated to fathom so saying 'I like you better than your friend' doesn't really tell them anything useful. Also, suggesting someone is making you feel something, such as 'You make me jealous' is a distortion because you have chosen to have that feeling, instead own up to your own feelings by saying, 'I feel jealous when...'.

I'd like to introduce you briefly to TA (Transactional Analysis). There are three states; parent, adult and child. We switch between these states all the time but relationships tend to work best when we are in 'adult' mode.

'Parent' is when we say things like 'You should' or 'You ought to' as if we are the parent. 'Child' is when we speak from our emotions such as 'I want'. Instead, move into 'adult' mode by expressing what you think and feel or observe.

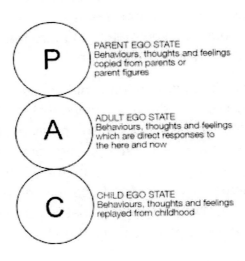

PARENT EGO STATE
Behaviours, thoughts and feelings copied from parents or parent figures

ADULT EGO STATE
Behaviours, thoughts and feelings which are direct responses to the here and now

CHILD EGO STATE
Behaviours, thoughts and feelings replayed from childhood

The ability to engage with your 'adult' mode is essential for issues around sex. The child in us wants to be loved and have physical contact and this is natural with someone we love and have a relationship with so long as you take precautions.

You may be pressured though by your girlfriend or boyfriend to do more than the 'adult' in you feels ready for. They may say things to persuade you such as 'if you loved me you'd sleep with me' or 'it doesn't feel as good with a condom'.

Decide for yourself when the time is right and make sure you have protected sex because Sexually Transmitted diseases (STDs) are a real risk and they are extremely unpleasant. Be sure to go straight to the GP if you think you might have one. They will treat you in confidence and they've seen everything so talk about it, there's no need to be shy or worry about it on your own.

Having sex with someone will not make them love you; in fact generally speaking the quicker you sleep with them, the sooner the relationship ends. Just because you kiss and 'make out' doesn't mean you have to have full on sex with them.

If you do something you don't feel comfortable with, you will lose respect for yourself and lose the respect of others you care about.

Respect yourself and do what's right for you by being 'internally referenced' (see the Identity chapter) that means asking yourself 'Does this feel right?' you will have the self esteem that will make you attractive to others as well as yourself.

Take time to get to know your boyfriend or girlfriend. No-one's first time is ever great so wait until you feel comfortable with them. We all feel self conscious being naked with the opposite sex, it's perfectly normal.

When you are in a long term relationship visit your GP because they will help you decide what precautions to take and they won't tell your parents.

Lastly, what you focus on is what you get so notice what you like in your girlfriend or boyfriend and that's what you'll get more of.

<u>CHAPTER 6. WORK</u>

Most teenagers are keen to work to earn money when they are still at school and if you have left school you may be looking for a job. We know how hard this can be so how can we improve our chances?

   1) Goal setting

Think about what you want to do. What are your strengths and skills (check out the confidence chapter) and take on board all that you have found out about yourself in the Identity chapter.

If you tend to think 'big chunk' you will need to chunk down to some detail about what specifically you want to do.

Use the Time Line to map out your future so you have a plan because that will impress whoever you approach for a job. State your objectives and career plan on your CV. List the skills and experience you already have in that area.

Apply for unpaid work experience that will build on those skills by asking teachers, friends of the family and people currently working in that career.

Research the career you are interested in and look for local companies that appeal to you. You can find all the information you need on the Internet.

   2) Put yourself in the employer's shoes

Dress to impress! Look the part you are applying for.

What is the company's mission statement, what is important to them and demonstrate that you are a good fit with it.

People like others who they think are similar to them. Listen to the interviewer's language pattern and match their visual, auditory or kinaesthetic language.

Match their volume, tone and pace by speaking in the same way. They won't notice it if you do it well but they will notice if you mismatch.

Match their body language too by sitting back if they are, sitting forward and mirror their facial expressions by smiling when they smile and looking serious when they do.

Have some questions ready, based perhaps on what you've read on their company website, particularly in the News or Press Release section.

Their map of the world is not yours so ask them what sort of person they are looking for, what is important to them.

3) The person with the most flexibility controls the system

By being flexible about what you want, chunking up perhaps if you've been very specific, you can get much needed experience in jobs that will eventually lead to what you are really after.

For example, babysitting shows you can handle responsibility, be punctual and reliable and have rapport with children and adults. These skills equip you for many other jobs. Look at the job that you are doing and list the skills you're using. Then add them to your CV in such a way that it demonstrates transferrable skills that could apply to other jobs.

Be flexible about what you earn. It may well be worthwhile to earn nothing in a job in order to be able to list the company or the skill on your CV. It may seem wrong to work for nothing but there is value in learning new skills if they are relevant to your goal.

4) There is no failure only feedback

You won't get every job you apply for but you can learn from your applications by contacting the interviewer or HR department and asking for feedback. Use the 'feedback sandwich' and ask what you did well, what would have been better and what was good overall. Apply what you have learnt to your next interview.

Remember if you always do what you've always done you will always get what you've always got

SO CHANGE WHAT YOU ARE DOING TO GET THE RESULT YOU WANT

AND FINALLY

If there is anything you are unsure about or would like to work on, please get in touch with me judy@nlpkids.com or via my website www.nlpkids.com and I would be happy to explain further or arrange an NLP coaching session.

References

Peter Jefford, Gemma Bailey and Sue Knight

– Brilliant Minds Telesummit 'NLP in action' January 2011

NLP at work, Sue Knight, Nicholas Brealey Publishing

The Satir Model, Virginia Satir, Science and Behavior Books

Lightning Source UK Ltd.
Milton Keynes UK
UKOW02f0009110417

298841UK00001B/81/P